Typical Devon cob at Marker's Cottage, Broadclyst, a National Trust property.

CLAY AND COB BUILDINGS

John McCann

Shire Publications Ltd

CONTENTS

Published in 1995 by Shire Publications Ltd, Cromwell House, Church Street, Princes Risborough, Buckinghamshire HP27 9AA, UK. Copyright © 1995 by John McCann. First published 1983; second edition 1995. Shire Album 105. ISBN 0 7478 0280 7.
John McCann is hereby identified as the author of this work in accordance with Section 77 of the Copyright, Designs and Patents Act 1988.

Printed in Great Britain by CIT Printing Services, Press Buildings, Merlins Bridge, Haverfordwest, Dyfed SA61 1XF.

British Library Cataloguing in Publication Data: McCann, John. Clay and Cob Buildings. – 2Rev.ed. – (Shire Albums; No.105). I. Title II. Series. 721.04422. ISBN 0-7478-0280-7.

ACKNOWLEDGEMENTS
The author wishes to express his gratitude to Martin Andrew, Dirk Bouwens, Veronica Chesher, Sylvia Colman, Beth Davis, Gordon Pearson, Eurwyn Wiliam, members of Devon Earth Building Association, the staff of Essex Record Office, and many others who have helped with local information or specialized knowledge. J. R. Harrison kindly read the draft text and made helpful suggestions. For more detailed studies the reader is referred to the Further reading chapter. Some illustrations are reproduced by kind permission of Essex Record Office, J. R. Harrison, and Bruce Walker, as indicated in the captions.
Except where otherwise stated the illustrations are by the author.

Cover: *Cottage of chalk cob at Orcheston, Wiltshire, with a base wall of brick, and with later brickwork at each side.*

Below: *A cob farmhouse at Sandford, Devon. Note the undulating surfaces and softly rounded corners. The external chimney is very typical of Devon. Many chimneys were added in the seventeenth century to houses built earlier; as prestigious features of their time they were proudly displayed at the front. The lean-to at the left is a later extension, also of cob.*

A cob cottage at Buxhall, Suffolk, built by the Reverend Copinger Hill for letting. This is an early type, with the upper rooms in the roof; in 1843 he specified that cottages must be of two full storeys. In 1839 this one was occupied by a wheelwright. An adjacent building of clay lump is visible on the left.

THE FOUR PROCESSES: COB, SHUTTERED EARTH, CLAY LUMP AND PISÉ

In many parts of Britain there are buildings made of unfired earth. They give a distinctive character to the architecture of the region, and they are comfortable to live in — warm in winter, cool in summer. They have been built of sub-soil containing clay or chalk by one of four processes — cob, shuttered earth, clay lump and *pisé*.

COB

This way of building is usually associated with the West Country, but under other names it has been used in many parts of Britain. The word *cob* is first recorded in Cornwall in 1602. The form *clob* was used in Berkshire in the eighteenth century, and the Welsh equivalent is *clom*. In Buckinghamshire the local form is called *witchert*, but elsewhere in Britain these buildings are usually described as *clay* or *mud*.

The traditional cob technique, sometimes called 'slow process', was well described in Suffolk by the Reverend Copinger Hill in 1843: 'Clay for building should be a clay-marl. If the clay is not good, chalk and road grit should be mixed with it .. with moderate clay, say seven-tenths clay, two-tenths chalk, one tenth road-grit. The clay and chalk are raised and carted to a convenient spot of hard

3

A cob cottage at Buxhall, Suffolk, of the type described by Copinger Hill in a prize essay in the Journal of the Royal Agricultural Society 1843. He advocated thatched roofs for the comfort of the tenants, but here the original thatch has been replaced later by asbestos tile. Note the deep window reveals. The upper right-hand window is original, of cast iron; the others are modern replacements. The original doorway is perceptible as an alteration in the texture of the plaster.

ground, where they are beaten to pieces by a heavy prong, and the stones picked out, and formed into a circular bed one foot thick and 20 feet in diameter (300 mm by 6 metres). The bed is well watered, and trodden by horses; and while trodden, one man shakes short straw upon it with a fork, while another pulls it about with the prong, and throws the outside portions under the feet of the horses, and supplies a sufficiency of water. It can hardly be too much trodden . . . It is then rounded up and covered with straw until wanted for use. When used it is somewhat moister than brick-earth prepared for moulding. A pinning (foundation wall) of stonework 14 inches (350 mm) thick and one foot (300 mm) out of the ground is prepared. One man gets upon the pinning with a small three-pronged fork; his partner throws up to him small lumps of clay, the size of a double-fist, which he adroitly catches on the fork, and deposits smartly on the wall, walking backwards. A height of 20 inches or 2 feet (500-600 mm) is built at one time; at intervals as the work proceeds the workmen coax the sides of the wall with spades and make it straight. It is then left to dry for a few days, or longer; all depends on the weather. When sufficiently dry another course is laid on till the requisite height is obtained. As the wall rises window-frames and door-frames are fixed; and when the roof is on the dauber with his trowel cases the walls inside and out with clay, corrects all defects and irregularities, and leaves it smooth and white. The clay for casing is prepared with more care than the body of the wall: old clay-wall worked up afresh makes the best casing.'

Similar descriptions from other parts of Britain show that the process was much the same everywhere. What differed (apart from the name) was the natural material available in each place. Chalk can be used pure, but clay soil must have aggregates — silt, sand and gravel. In some places all the required aggregates are naturally present, but elsewhere the coarser aggregates have to be added. Cob builders developed and passed on the traditional skills of judging the composition of the local soil and selecting the aggregates necessary to form good building material. Large quantities of straw (or in some places rushes or heather) were mixed in to provide fibrous reinforcement and to minimise shrinkage cracks.

Most cob walls were thicker than those described by Copinger Hill. Ancient farmhouses in Devon have cob walls 3 feet (900 mm) or more thick, but 20-24 inches (500-600 mm) is more common. Some diminish in thickness above joist level, presenting a vertical surface outside. The height of the 'rises' or courses varies with different material, according to how high it would stand without slumping. Also, the courses may be of different heights in one building, perhaps indicating that work was interrupted by rain, or that it was done in the intervals between other jobs. Chimneys may be of cob or stone; by

Right: *Typical Devon cob in the gable end of a barn at Spreyton. It is not unusual to see courses of different heights in the same building. The modern roof gives less protection to the walls than traditional thatch with a long overhang, and consequently the cob is much eroded by rainwater. The vertical scar indicates where an adjoining building has been removed.*

Below: *A boundary wall of witchert at Haddenham, Buckinghamshire. The plinth is built of coursed stone rubble. The coping would have been of thatch originally, later replaced by tiles.*

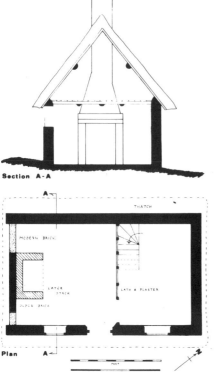

Section A-A

Plan

Above and left: Recorded in the last stage of decay in 1977, this cottage at Kettlebaston, Suffolk, was a typical farm labourer's dwelling of the early nineteenth century. Three exactly regular walls 13 inches (330 mm) thick were formed of puddled clay to eaves level. Above the clay walling the right gable was of lath and plaster. The left end consisted originally of a brick chimney stack with the spaces to each side infilled with lath and plaster. There was only one upper room, at the right end, and this was wholly in the roof.

now the upper part has usually been rebuilt in brickwork.

Contemporary records show that cob buildings were erected quite quickly. Sometimes the sub-soil was excavated before winter and left out for the frost to act upon it, but laying on the courses could not begin until spring. The walls reached full height in one season, and the roof was added before winter. In 1911 Ernest Gimson built a substantial house of two full storeys at Budleigh Salterton, Devon; eight men completed the cob walls in three months.

6

Well-made cob will last indefinitely if it is protected from the wet. The normal humidity of moist air does not affect it, but if it is allowed to become saturated it reverts to a plastic condition and collapses. A foundation wall of masonry, the higher the better, was used to raise the cob above the reach of rising damp and rain-splash. Traditional buildings did not have gutters; rain was thrown clear by long overhanging eaves. Houses of cob were lime-plastered or lime-washed — at least at the front; frequently renewed, coat on coat, eventually the limewash comes to resemble lime plaster. Many farm buildings and boundary walls were left without any protective coating.

SHUTTERED EARTH

Puddled clay and *puddled chalk* are variants of this layered construction. The masonry plinth was built as before, and the material was prepared in much the same way. Wooden shuttering was erected on the plinth, and the material was shovelled in and trampled down in shallow layers until the void was filled. The shuttering was left in position until the material was dry enough to support itself and then was moved up to form another course. The advantages of this method were: (1) material which was too sloppy for normal cob technique could be used; (2) the walls could be made thinner than when built freehand; (3) perfectly vertical surfaces and geometrical corners were easily formed.

CLAY LUMP (also called clay bat)

In this method the clay-straw mixture was formed into rectangular blocks which were laid in courses like modern concrete blocks. The process was described in 1842 by John Curtis of Rougham, Norfolk. Soft yellow clay, without the addition of chalk or grit, was mixed with water and straw and trodden by horses, as already described. 'As soon as the clay is properly prepared men should make it up into lumps, which is done by putting sufficient clay into a mould of wood, of the following dimensions: 18 inches long, 12 inches wide, and 6 inches deep (450 by 300 by 150 mm) without a bottom. The mould, when well filled by the men putting in the clay with a spade, and pressing it with the foot, the top being smoothed with the spade, should be lifted up, and the lump will be left perfect. Wet the mould with a wisp of oat straw to prevent the clay hanging to it, and place the mould about 2 inches (50 mm) from the first lump, and fill as before .... This filling of the mould is best done on level grass ground. As soon as the lumps get a little stiff, that is, just enough to admit of handling them, they should be set on one edge, and as they dry be turned; and in doing this place the wet side in the sun.' When firm enough to be lifted the blocks were loosely stacked to dry. 'Winter is the best time to get the clay into heaps, that the frost may pulverize and mellow it. In March, as soon as the severe frosts are over, begin to work the clay and make the lumps, and if the weather be favourable they will be fit to build with in three weeks or a month.'

The size of the blocks varies, but usually they are smaller than those described by Curtis, typically 18 inches long by 9 inches wide by 6 inches deep (450 by 225 by 150 mm). In most parts of East Anglia there is no good building stone, so the

A wooden mould for making clay lumps, and some used clay lumps, showing how much the material may differ from one area to another. Collected in Norfolk by Dirk Bouwens

Clay lumps of moist clay-straw mixture pressed into a wooden mould and dried naturally. They were laid with clay mortar, as shown at right. At Chapel End, Broxted, Essex.

foundation wall was built of flints, field stones or brickwork, with lime mortar. The clay lumps were laid on it in stretcher bond, using finer clay material as mortar. External walls would be 9 inches (225 mm) thick, but for internal partitions the blocks were laid on edge to form walls 6 inches (150 mm) thick. Some clay lump cottages have brick chimneys, but many have chimneys of clay lump to roof level, with brickwork above. Originally the walls of cottages were coated with smooth clay containing chopped straw, but by now most of them have been rendered with lime plaster. If the render is intact a cottage of clay lump is difficult to distinguish from one of solid brickwork. Many farm buildings of clay lump were protected externally by gas tar or sprayed bitumen.

There was a substantial technical advantage in using clay-bound sub-soil in blocks because it largely solved the problem of shrinkage. All clay soils expand when moistened and shrink as they dry; a continuous wall of expansive clay tended to form shrinkage cracks as it dried. If the aggregates were insufficient or poorly selected a major failure might result. The clays of East Anglia are particularly expansive, and the aggregates naturally present in the sub-soil rarely form an ideal mixture for building. The advantages of using the material in blocks were: (1) the sub-soil available on site could be used without adding aggregates; (2) most of the shrinkage occurred before the blocks were incorporated in the building; (3) the separate blocks dried more quickly than a solid wall; (4) building could proceed continuously; (5) the thinner walls required less material.

Clay lump had other advantages which had more to do with the stylistic taste of the nineteenth century. Improving landlords were demolishing shabby and unhealthy cottages, poorly built on minimal foundations, with irregular lines and rounded corners. They chose to replace

8

Buildings of clay lump are very difficult to recognise when they are plastered. Here, two cottages built in the early nineteenth century at Hatfield Broad Oak, Essex, were converted into one house in 1973. The original doorways were blocked and new apertures made for modern windows. The clay lumps were found to be in excellent condition and were re-used with modern breeze blocks to fill the old apertures. The block size is shown most clearly in the gable wall; in the front wall it is confused by grooves cut to key the plaster.

Clay lump cottages at Birdbrook, Essex, deteriorating through lack of maintenance. Rain pouring down the walls from leaking gutters has washed away the surface of the clay. Where the rendering has fallen away the floor joists are visible, laid on a plank incorporated in the wall to spread the load. The chimney at the right is of clay lump up to roof level, with brickwork above.

them with cottages which were visually distinct from the old — of rectangular design, with straight vertical walls and sharp arrises. Clay lump naturally lent itself to the desired architectural style.

D. Bouwens has shown that the amount of straw incorporated varied greatly, but the lumps containing most straw are strongest and most resistant to weathering. Like cob, clay lump will tolerate a considerable degree of overall humidity, but if it becomes saturated locally it will collapse. Defective roofs and guttering allow water to soak into the material, reducing it to a plastic state.

PISÉ (or rammed earth)

The *pisé* process was entirely different, in that the available sub-soil was used almost dry, without straw or other fibre, and was heavily rammed in shallow layers within shuttering so that it consolidated immediately, effectively forming artificial rock. Layers were added and rammed, without intervals for drying, until the walls reached full height. The process depended on a specially designed wooden frame (see opposite), strongly constructed to resist the great pressure of ramming, which could be dismantled and moved along as each section was completed. The end of one section of rammed earth was ramped and overlaid by the next, and the joints were staggered. The shuttering was blocked vertically to form door and window apertures, and lintels and fixing blocks were built in as the work advanced. The holes left by the putlogs or transverse ties were filled, and after a period of drying the walls were finished with lime plaster outside and inside.

A *pisé* building can be identified only when the plaster is removed. The fabric differs from cob or 'slow process' shuttered earth in that it is harder and denser, and it does not contain any vegetable fibre. Regular horizontal lines of putlog holes about 3 feet (900 mm) apart may be visible in the material itself and in the top of the plinth.

(Turf walling, and variant forms of earth walling in which mud was integrated with light timberwork, as in the 'mud and stud' cottages of Lincolnshire and the 'daubed palisade' buildings of north-east Scotland, are outside the scope of this Album.)

Above: *This farm at Southburgh, Norfolk, consists almost entirely of clay lump buildings on brick plinths. Some of the tar applied for weather protection has fallen away.*

Below: *Illustrations of the equipment used for building in pisé, published by Johnson and Cresey in 1847, but evidently adapted from Henry Holland's engravings of 1797. The strongly-made shuttering could be dismantled and moved along as each section was completed. The iron tie rod on the right would have held the posts more rigidly than the 'Spanish windlass' type of tie illustrated on the left. The heart-shaped hardwood rammer was advocated by Cointeraux. The central block forms vertical ends to the pisé for door and window apertures.*

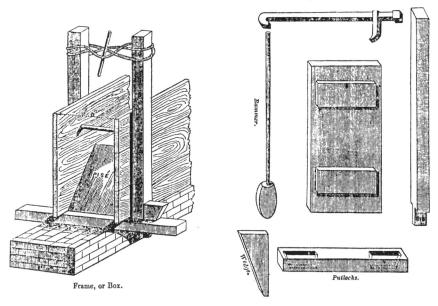

Frame, or Box.

11

Section y.e 5th a nother Cottage Built for y.e Smallest Quantity of money
as possible y.e length 32 feet weadth 16 foott from out to out and y.e height to y.e
over way is 12 foot Done with Clay wall cover'd over lime & hair And rended over
with lime and hair within Side on Stack of Chimneys Earth floor And Two Chambers
4 window in y.e front and 2 windows at Each End plaster'd with lime & hair between y.e pars,
in y.e Chambers Chamer floors laid with Elm or fir: all y.e Spars tops y.e of a Tree And y.e
girders girting Inches 16 foot & half long all y.e Timber large boughs

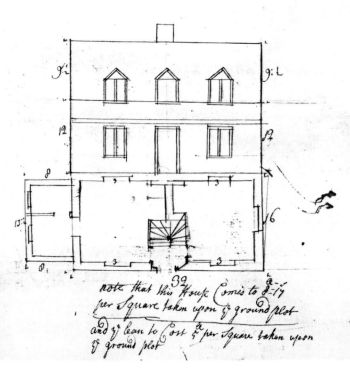

note that this House Comes to £-19
per Square taken upon y.e ground plot
and y.e lean to Cost £.a per Square taken upon
y.e ground plot

The design and specification of a 'Cottage Built for the Smallest Quantity of money as possible' by James Deane of Colchester. It is undated but he lived from 1699 to 1765. 'Done with Clay wall covered over (with) lime and hair and rended (rendered) over with lime and hair within.' The type of clay construction was not specified. By courtesy of Essex Record Office.

THE ORIGIN AND HISTORY OF EARTH WALLING

Mud is one of the oldest building materials. Some of the simplest dwellings in the world are made by weaving pliant rods together to form a basket-like structure, and daubing it with mud mixed with fibrous matter. A similar material, wattle and daub, is found in timber-framed buildings in Britain, but there it is used as panels of infill in a timber structure. In these buildings the wooden components provide most of the strength, but in cob, shuttered earth, clay lump and *pisé* the material has its own compressive strength, requiring timber only to bridge over door and window apertures, and for roofs and floors.

Unfired bricks of mud and straw over six thousand years old have been excavated at Hassuna in Iraq, and similar material has been found in many other ancient cultures. These early bricks were roughly shaped by hand, more rounded than rectangular. In the first century BC Vitruvius described the manufacture of unfired bricks of shallow rectangular shape containing straw, and specified how they should be laid. Pliny described the *pisé* process in Spain and north Africa in the first century AD.

In dry climates archaeological evidence of earth construction is recoverable, but in the wetter conditions of Britain these buildings tend to revert to earth soon after they are abandoned. At Verulamium, St Albans, Hertfordshire, S. S. Frere has excavated Roman walls of 'clean yellow clay' formed between boards on a stone foundation, with putlog holes at intervals of 8 feet (2.44 metres), what we now describe as *puddled clay*. Low walls of clay packed between shuttering of wattle, dating from the Viking period, have been excavated at York, and other early earth-walled structures have been excavated in London, Norwich and elsewhere.

The place-name Mudwall is recorded in London from 1395, and in Essex from 1497. The Welsh name Pontypridd means 'the bridge by the earthen house'. In 1540 John Leland described the fortifications of King Henry VIII's naval base at Portsmouth as 'a mudde wall armid with timbre'; the wall supported artillery. The great strength of mud fortifications must have been in John Locke's mind in 1690 when he wrote: 'Earthly minds, like Mud-Walls, resist the strongest batteries.'

COB AND SHUTTERED EARTH

There are references to buildings of mud or clay in historic records of all periods, but they tell us little about the processes used. Most writers regarded the dwellings of the common people as unworthy of comment. From the late eighteenth century humanitarian reformers became concerned about the squalid conditions in which most farmworkers lived and brought up their children. They tried to persuade landed gentlemen that it was in their interest to build improved cottages for their tenants. The movement had little effect until the 1790s, and then only in 'closed parishes', where one landlord owned all the land and could control the tenancies. In 'open parishes' where ownership was more dispersed there was resistance from ratepayers who feared that providing better cottages would attract more people into the parish, and so increase the poor rate. The Poor Law Amendment Act of 1834 established Unions of parishes and Union workhouses, and ended this objection. Cottages sprang up everywhere. In 1843 the Reverend Copinger Hill wrote in Suffolk: 'Cottages are too much in the hands of speculators, who exact an exorbitant rent for very inferior accommodation'. He and other housing reformers showed that it was possible to provide well-built cottages, with two rooms downstairs and two bedrooms above, at rents which farmworkers could afford. In the early nineteenth century architects and land agents produced a large literature on cottage building which provides us now with good contemporary descriptions of all the earth-building processes then in use.

A tax on bricks from 1784, which increased their cost by about 15 per cent, provided an additional incentive to look at earth building techniques. The material cost only the wages for digging, and no fuel was consumed. There was little or no expenditure on carting, for the sub-soil was extracted near the building site. A pond at the end of a cottage garden usually indicates where the material came from. In the model cottages described by Copinger Hill in 1843 clay walls cost £17, while stone walls cost £39 plus cartage from the quarry. Brickwork was even more expensive; he recommended it only for chimneys and ovens.

CLAY LUMP (or clay bat)

This method of building has long been used in drier climates elsewhere in the world, but in Britain it was a late development. Authors writing before 1987 asserted that it was a traditional method of building in Norfolk and Suffolk, and claimed to identify ancient farmhouses there of clay lump. More recent research has shown this to be a fallacy; no standing buildings of clay lump in Britain earlier than the nineteenth century have been confirmed.

In the eighteenth century thin *bats* of chalky clay mixed with straw were used to form the nest-boxes of dovecotes, where the main structure was of other materials; it was thought that clay and chalk were more attractive to the birds than hard stone or brick. An ingenious bricklayer named Joseph Austin, who had made clay bats for dovecotes, conceived the idea of using them to build himself a cottage. As far as is known his cottage at Great Shelford, Cambridgeshire, begun in June 1791, was the first building in England *structurally composed* of clay bats.

James Plumptree, a housing reformer, published an account of this innovation in 1801. By 1820 many cottages and ancillary buildings of clay bats had been built in Cambridgeshire; probably Joseph Austin and his large family of sons and nephews, who were all bricklayers, were responsible for spreading the technique. Another social reformer, John Denson, published an account of the method in 1821, and subsequently built himself a cottage at Waterbeach; he used the term *clay lumps*. In 1833 J. C. Loudon reprinted Denson's text in his *Encyclopaedia of Cottage, Farm and Villa Architecture*, and

Cob cottages at Broadclyst, Devon

Nest boxes for dovecotes were formed of chalky clay bats long before the material was used structurally in Britain. Here the bats are 2 ¹/₂ inches (65 mm) thick.

described it as a Cambridgeshire technique. It was revised and republished many times, and was immensely influential. John Curtis's longer description of the process as practised in Norfolk (quoted above) first appeared in the edition of 1847.

In the 1830s and 1840s an agricultural revolution was in progress in Norfolk and Suffolk. The heavy clay lands which formerly had been used as pasture were being drained and converted to arable. Whole farmsteads were rebuilt, and many new cottages were required. Where coastal and river transport was available the agricultural 'improvers' used established materials, but further inland, where carting was expensive, they were glad to adopt the new clay lump process. That is why more buildings of clay lump are found in south Norfolk and north-west Suffolk than anywhere else. A similar innovation was reported in Perthshire in 1792, but the clay lump process was not adopted there on a comparable scale.

PISÉ

Pisé was a traditional form of construction in the Rhône valley of France, in parts of Spain, and in north Africa, where the soils and climate are particularly suitable; it is still practised in Morocco. In 1772 G. C. Goiffon described the process in *L'Art du Maçon Piseur*. From 1791 François Cointeraux took it up and produced a series of technical manuals which were widely influential. In 1795 the fifth Duke of Bedford and his architect Henry Holland introduced the process in Woburn park and in estate cottages nearby. Holland published an English translation of Cointeraux's instructions in *Communications to the Board of Agriculture* of 1797, specifically recommending it for farmworkers' cottages. Because *pisé* was introduced at this high social level it was described with enthusiasm by others; the architectural literature of the early nineteenth century includes numerous accounts of the process. Careful reading reveals that most of those who wrote about it had never used it, and were merely rehashing Holland's text and illustrations. The *pisé* process was adopted successfully for gentry houses in Hampshire, where the chalky soil is ideally suitable. To make other types of soil consolidate by dry ramming required arduous and unremitting labour, closely supervised. Instructions for building with *pisé* continued to be copied from book to book (disregarding some failures) to the 1860s. *Pisé* was never part of the vernacular building tradition in Britain.

In 1850 the Brick Tax was abolished, and from the 1860s the brick industry became increasingly mechanized. The

An architect-designed estate cottage of clay lump built in 1904 at Elsenham, Essex, with original cladding of weatherboards. Others here, formerly of identical design, have been altered by removing the weatherboards and roughcasting and by adding extensions.

main railway network had been completed, and cheap bricks could be transported from distant sources. Architectural taste turned away from the old methods; an industrial society increasingly favoured the use of industrial products. In many rural areas, and the towns generally, building with mud or cob was wholly superseded by brickwork. Improved supplies of lime, brought by rail, encouraged building with stone rubble where cob had been common earlier. From 1875 arable farming areas fell into deep depression owing to imports of cheap grain from north America, and a decade later stock-farming areas were almost equally affected by imports of refrigerated meat. Farmworkers left the land to seek work in the towns or to emigrate, and the building of rural cottages almost ceased. By the time building was resumed brick had become the accepted building material.

In rural Devon, where the cob tradition was strongest, domestic buildings were mainly built of stone by the second half of the nineteenth century. Agricultural buildings, too, were built more in stone, often with dressings of brick, but cob was cheaper and its use continued on a reduced scale. Shuttering techniques were increasingly employed, probably to conform with changing architectural taste. The need to keep the thousands of existing cob buildings in repair helped to prevent the traditional craft knowledge from dying out.

In Buckinghamshire the use of witchert (a local form of cob) continued until the end of the nineteenth century. In south Norfolk clay lump remained in favour, many of the later buildings being faced with fired bricks. In 1904 Sir Walter Gilbey built superior cottages of clay lump clad with weatherboards on his estate at Elsenham, Essex, but by 1912 he had turned to brickwork.

16

A cob cottage at North Petherwin, Cornwall, with a hipped roof of Cornish slate. The south-west wall, which receives most of the heavy rain, is protected by hung slates.

THE REGIONAL PATTERN

COB

The largest concentration of cob buildings in Britain extends across the south-western counties from Cornwall to Hampshire. Devon has most of all, estimated in tens of thousands. Manor houses and farmhouses of cob survive from the fourteenth century, with archaeological evidence from the twelfth century. Farm buildings of cob survive from all periods. Fashionable villas for the gentry, and even four-storeyed town houses, continued to be built of cob until the middle of the nineteenth century. The material varies greatly in colour, from deep red and red-brown on the Permian Sandstones to grey on the Culm Measures. Cob is closely integrated with the traditional culture of the region, accepted at all social levels. The skill of the local practitioners must command our respect, for the geology of Devon is complex, and the cob process was used successfully with

widely different soils. As one proceeds eastwards across Dorset, Wiltshire and Hampshire one encounters more chalky soils; the cob buildings are creamy white. Chalk cob — particularly as boundary walls — may be found wherever there are chalky soils.

A particular form of 'slow process' material known as *witchert* (spelled variously, but probably derived from 'white earth') occurs in Buckinghamshire and Oxfordshire, in a belt extending from east of Aylesbury through Thame to Dorchester. There the high content of chalk in the clay sub-soil makes it ideally suitable for this technique. Courses may be built 3 feet (900 mm) high without slumping, and walls of this material will stand to a height of 20 feet (6 metres) or more.

There is another concentration of 'slow process' buildings in Leicestershire, Northamptonshire, and eastern Warwick-

Above: *Haddenham Baptist Church, Buckinghamshire, built of witchert but to a strictly formal design with crisp outlines. The height of the walls indicates the extraordinary stability of this local form of cob.*
Below: *Witchert garden walls are to be seen everywhere at Haddenham. The plinth of coursed rubble is clearly shown here; the render is modern but is well executed to retain the traditional appearance.*

Above: *The lodge of Maddington Manor, Wiltshire, built in Gothick style in the early nineteenth century. The boundary wall of creamy white chalk mud sweeps gracefully up to meet it and retains the traditional coping of thatch.*

Below: *Two cottages and a spur wall of chalk cob at Rockbourne, Hampshire, photographed in 1982, altered since. Because a gable wall of cob could be unstable it was built in cob only to eaves level, and continued up to the roof with timber framing. Note the tiled sills under the dormers to protect the cob from rain.*

Above: *The village of Milton Abbas, Dorset, was demolished and re-sited about 1790 as part of a major landscaping scheme to improve the view from the house of the squire, Joseph Dormer. The architect of the new model village is believed to have been Sir William Chambers. The cottages were built in attached pairs, of cob with roofs of heather thatch, but are now combined.*

Below: *A garden wall of chalk cob at Ashwell, Hertfordshire, on a base wall of flint rubble. The traditional thatch coping is present, but what used to be a cheap covering has become an expensive material to maintain.*

shire. The material is known locally as *mud*, yellowish brown in colour, formed from the Liassic sub-soil; mostly it is built on high foundation walls of stone rubble of similar colour. The mud walling rarely stands more than 10 feet (3 metres) above the plinth. Boundary walls and farm buildings are most common, left unrendered, but also there are cottages and small farmhouses, mostly lime-plastered and thatched; many have corrugated iron over the thatch. There are many examples in Great Dalby, Billesdon, Harby and Saddington. In this area the gentry houses are of stone, and the mud buildings never commanded the same re-

Right: *This small farmhouse at Great Creaton, Northamptonshire, has side walls of mud but exhibits a stone gable where it is most visible. Although mud is a sound building material it has long been regarded there as inferior to stone.*

Below: *This farmhouse is the last remaining dwelling built of mud at Nether Broughton, Leicestershire, although mud construction used to be common there. Originally it was a low building with the upper rooms partly in the roof; it has been raised with brickwork to accommodate a full upper storey.*

spect; most of those which survive are badly patched with modern bricks and cement, or otherwise deteriorating. The boundary walls were thatched originally, but now most have copings of corrugated iron or tiles. Farm buildings, too, were formerly protected by long overhanging roofs of thatch, but they have been re-roofed with slate, with a minimal over-hang. Rainwater is discharged on to the walls, causing progressive erosion.

Another group of clay farmhouses, cottages and farm buildings, known locally as *clay dabbins*, occurs in the Solway Plain of Cumberland. They were described in 1962 by R. W. Brunskill, and more recently have been considered in greater detail by J. R. Harrison, as listed under 'Further reading'. Here a different method of building was used, which Dr Brunskill called 'quick process'. Shallow layers of mud, only 3-4 inches (75-100 mm) thick, were built up continu-ously on high base walls of cobbles and clay mortar. Straw was not mixed with the mud but was laid over each layer to form a bed for the next.

Contemporary accounts describe a whole community coming together to build the main walls of a house for a newly married couple in one day. Much of the weight of the thatched roof was taken by horizontal timbers supported on crucks; the feet of the rafters rested freely on the side walls. The earliest clay dabbins which survive date from the late seventeenth century; most are of the eighteenth or early nineteenth centuries. Mostly they are now much altered with stone and cement render, or disused and derelict. There are reports that a similar 'quick process' has been used in Devon, but little physical evidence has been found.

In Wales, although good building stone is available in most areas, mud was used

A ruined clay dabbin farmhouse at Kelsick on the Solway Plain, Cumberland, photographed in 1979, since destroyed. The typical thin beds of clay are separated from each other by layers of straw. The roof would have been thatched originally, later replaced by slates. Photograph by J. R. Harrison.

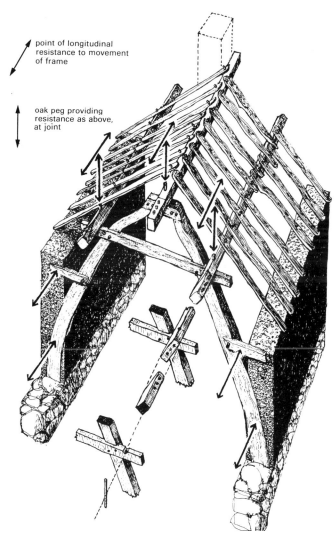

point of longitudinal
resistance to movement
of frame

oak peg providing
resistance as above,
at joint

Three-dimensional diagram of a typical clay dabbin farmhouse of the Solway Plain, showing how most of the weight of the thatched roof is carried by crucks supporting a ridge-piece and purlins without transmitting much weight to the side walls, and how the construction resists longitudinal stresses. Drawing by J. R. Harrison.

extensively for cottages in the nineteenth century, and for farmhouses and farm buildings earlier. The material varies from yellow clay to grey mud containing flakes of stone, built up in layers of various depths on base walls which are always of stone. Often mud and stone are combined in various ways. Single-storey cottages may have stone quoins and stone dressings round windows and door in the front elevation, with all the rest comprised of mud. Gable-end chimneys may be of mud up to roof level, or some chimneys were made wholly of wicker. Although building with mud has been widely practised in Wales the distribution of surviving buildings is entirely western. There are examples in many parts of Dyfed, with concentrations in west Carmarthen and the Aeron valley, and a smaller number

Above: *A derelict nineteenth-century cottage at Esgair, Dyfed. The quoins and foundation wall are of stone, the rest of mud. The walls are 2 feet (600 mm) thick, with a chimney entirely of mud up to roof level. Many Welsh cottages had a cowhouse, as here, also built of mud.*
Below: *A mud cottage at Crugau Bach, Roshirwaun, in the Lleyn peninsula of Gwynedd. The stone plinth is visible below the lime-washed mud walling.*

A cottage and ruined shop of clay and bool at Bogmuir, Moray, with a detail of the construction. Drawings by Bruce Walker.

in the Lleyn peninsula of Gwynedd. In most areas mud cottages are now abandoned, but some are occupied and well maintained.

In Scotland Alexander Fenton and Bruce Walker have shown that there is a long tradition of building with clay in all the eastern counties from Sutherland to Fife. The cob process is usually called *clay dab*. In Galloway and Dumfriesshire clay buildings similar to those of Cumberland were formerly common, but very few have survived.

SHUTTERED EARTH

Buildings and boundary walls of puddled clay are common in Norfolk and present in Suffolk. Most standing buildings of puddled clay date from the early nineteenth century. Puddled chalk is common in Hampshire and Wiltshire, where it may be difficult to distinguish

from true *pisé*. In north-east Scotland there were variant techniques such as *clay and bool*, in which stones of similar size were laid in clay-straw mixture against the inside of shuttering. The finished wall presents an external appearance of regular courses or herringbone patterns. Eventually a technique was developed in Perthshire in which stone or brick walling was used to form the outer skin for puddled clay construction, and was left permanently in place. There are houses in the main street of Errol which have front elevations of brickwork (the most fashionable material when built) and side and rear elevations of stone rubble, but which consist mainly of clay-straw mixture.

CLAY LUMP AND CLAY BAT

Nineteenth-century cottages of *clay bats* — the local name — are quite

25

common in Cambridgeshire and north-west Essex, but they are difficult to recognise without detailed examination because the material is concealed by lime plaster outside and inside. The earliest ones are built with shallow 'bats' 3-4 inches (75-100 mm) deep. The largest concentration of clay lump buildings occurs in south Norfolk and north-west Suffolk, for the economic reasons already given. There clay lump was used for buildings of all kinds — including schools, public buildings and industrial buildings. Cottages of clay lump occur elsewhere in Essex, Hertfordshire and Bedfordshire, seldom other types of buildings, because the same economic conditions did not occur there at the same time. Landowners read of the process in Loudon's *Encyclopaedia* and other printed works, and tried it on a small scale; isolated examples have been found in other counties.

These are the main concentrations of earth buildings in Britain which still stand today, but historical records and occasional survivals show that earth has been used as a building material in many other areas, even where good building stone was available. The changeover from clay to stone construction can usually be related to tenants acquiring secure tenure, to enhanced agricultural prosperity, or to the introduction of new industries to an area.

PISÉ

The *pisé* process was not as successful in Britain as contemporary architectural literature might suggest. G. Pearson has shown that *pisé*, and English variants of it, were adopted by the main building industry for gentry houses in Hampshire and Wiltshire. In Winchester he relates its use to railway construction, which produced large amounts of surplus chalk. Outside the chalk belt of southern England *pisé* buildings are extremely rare.

A block of four clay lump cottages at Birdbrook, Essex, built about 1835. The plinth is of flint rubble and one course of brickwork, painted with tar. The furthest two cottages have been combined to form one house; modern plaster and modern windows give it a totally different appearance from the others.

Above: *Two witchert cottages of one and a half storeys at Haddenham, Buckinghamshire. Note the softly rounded arris in the foreground. The taller Victorian house beyond is also of witchert.*
Below: *Part of a remarkable group of cottages at Dunchurch, Warwickshire, built by the cob process but known locally as 'mud', protected by plaster. The base wall and corners are of brickwork. Note the deep window reveals.*

Lower Tricombe Farm, Northleigh, Devon, showing the new cob wing built by Kevin McCabe in 1993. The red-brown cob is still exposed, almost ready for rendering.

MODERN REVIVALS OF EARTH BUILDING

The substantial merits of earth buildings have led to a number of attempts to revive them in Britain. Fortunately the knowledge of how to build with earth has never wholly died out. Ernest Gimson was consciously reviving an earlier vernacular when he used cob to build an Arts and Crafts movement house in Devon in 1911,

but he found a local builder who remembered the techniques from having practised them thirty years earlier. During the First World War J. St. Loe Strachey experimented with *pisé* for some minor buildings at Newlands Corner, Surrey, where the soil is chalk. After the war Clough Williams-Ellis campaigned to reintroduce all the earth-building processes to meet the massive deficiency of conventional building materials and transport. Council houses of clay lump were built at Attleborough, Blo' Norton, East Harling, Garboldisham, Hepworth, Watton and elsewhere in mid Norfolk. A government body, the Building Research Board, used the various earth-walling techniques to build experimental cottages at Amesbury, Wiltshire. As a proportion of the national economy the post-war revival of earth building proved to be negligible, but Williams-Ellis's more important contribution was to keep the knowledge alive when it might have been lost

After the Second World War another shortage of building materials occurred, and J. and E. Eastwick-Field revised and re-issued Williams-Ellis's book. They had no more success in influencing the building industry. The reasons are clear. In the early nineteenth century, when the cottage-building movement was at its height, economic conditions were favourable to earth building. Handmade bricks were inherently expensive, and in addition they were taxed. In many districts supplies of wood fuel for burning bricks and lime were inadequate. Where water transport was not available it was expensive to bring in building materials or coal from distant sources. The rural work force was chronically under-employed, and labour was cheap. By 1919, or 1947, all these conditions had ceased to apply.

The future of earth building on a major scale now lies outside Britain. There are many countries where the high cost of imported fuel, the difficulties of transport, the low cost of labour and a pressing need for simple housing recall the economic state of early nineteenth-century Britain. The earth-building technologies have been improved by scientific analysis, machinery has been developed (for instance, for making compressed earth blocks) and con-struction is expanding rapidly overseas. In Britain there has been a revival of the traditional methods in recent years, but it has taken a different form, con-centrating on repairing the great number of neglected historic buildings of unfired earth. The Devon Historic Buildings Trust and the Devon Earth Building Association have published technical papers on repairing cob buildings, and the latter arranges seminars. EARTHA, founded in 1994, is pursuing similar aims in East Anglia. An Earth Structures Group of the international organisation ICOMOS has been established in Britain, and training in the conservation of earth buildings has become established at York and Plymouth Universities. From 1990 a few new buildings of cob have been built in Devon (see opposite). There is a growing corps of architects, surveyors and builders experienced in the earth-building technologies, and some local authorities are becoming familiar with the technical requirements.

Apart from Marker's Cottage, Broadclyst, Devon, which belongs to the National Trust, all the buildings illustrated in this book are privately owned; they are not open to the public. As internal surfaces are plastered there is rarely anything to see of the construction inside.

Above: *A boundary wall and farmhouse of cob at Cheriton Fitzpaine, Devon. Note the cob chimney stack. In both cases the traditional thatched roofs have been replaced by modern materials.*
Below: *The Post Office, Great Dalby, Leicestershire, built of mud with a thatched roof, but covered with corrugated iron to reduce maintenance costs.*

FURTHER READING

Andrew, M. 'Walls with Hats On: Witchert Buildings of Buckinghamshire', *Country Life*, 2nd October 1986, 1014-5.

Beacham, P. (editor). *Devon Building: an Introduction to Local Traditions*. Devon Books, Exeter, 1990.

Bouwens, D. 'Clay Lump in South Norfolk: Observations and Recollections', *Vernacular Architecture*, volume 19 (1988), 10-18.

Brunskill, R. W. 'The Clay Houses of Cumberland', *Transactions of the Ancient Monuments Society*, volume 10 n.s. (1962), 57-80.

Building Research Board report number 5, *Building in Cob, Clay Lump and Pisé de Terre*. HMSO, 1922.

Devon Historic Buildings Trust and Devon Earth Building Association. Advisory papers on conserving cob buildings issued from 1992 onwards.

Egeland, P. *Cob and Thatch*. Devon Books, Exeter, 1988.

Fenton, A. 'Clay Building and Clay Thatch in Scotland', *Ulster Folklife*, volume 15/16 (1970), 28-51.

Frere, S. S. 'Excavations at Verulamium, 1956, Second Interim Report', *Antiquaries Journal*, volume 37 (January-April 1957), 1-15.

Harrison, J. R. 'The Mud Wall in England at the Close of the Vernacular Era', *Transactions of the Ancient Monuments Society*, volume 28 n.s. (1984), 155-74.

Harrison, J. R. 'Some Clay Dabbins in Cumberland: Their Construction and Form', *Transactions of the Ancient Monuments Society*, volumes 33 n.s. (1989), 97-151, and 35 (1991), 29-88.

Hill, C. 'On the Construction of Cottages', *Journal of the Royal Agricultural Society*, (1843), 356-69.

Holland, H. 'On Cottages', *Appendix to Communications to the Board of Agriculture*, volume 1 (London, 1797), 377-403.

Jaggard, W. R. *Experimental Cottages: a Report on the Work of the Department at Amesbury, Wiltshire*. Department of Scientific and Industrial Research. HMSO, 1922.

Johnson, C. W., and Cresey, E. *On the Cottages of Agricultural Labourers* (1847), 44-52.

McCann, J. 'Is Clay Lump a Traditional Building Material?', *Vernacular Architecture*, volume 18 (1987), 1-16.

McCann, J. 'The First Cottage of Clay Bats?', *Proceedings of the Cambridge Antiquarian Society*, volume 76 (1987), 113-21.

McCann, J. 'Warm in Winter, Cool in Summer: Mud Buildings of the East Midlands', *Country Life*, 11th November 1982, 1472-3.

Norton, J. *Building with Earth, a Handbook*. IT Publications, Rugby, 1986.

Pearson, G. *Conservation of Clay and Chalk Buildings*. Donhead, London, 1992.

Seaborne, M. V. B. 'Cob Cottages in Northamptonshire', *Northamptonshire Past and Present*, volume 3 number 5 (1964), 215-28.

Vitruvius. *The Ten Books of Architecture*, translated by M. H. Morgan. Dover Publications, New York, 1960, 42-4.

Walker, B. *Clay Buildings in North-east Scotland*. Scottish Vernacular Buildings Working Group, Dundee and Edinburgh, 1977.

Wiliam, E. *Home-made Homes: Dwellings of the Rural Poor in Wales*. National Museum of Wales, Cardiff, 1988.

Williams-Ellis, C. *Cottage Building in Cob, Pisé, Chalk and Clay*. Country Life, London, 1919.

Williams-Ellis, C., and Eastwick-Field, J. and E. *Building in Cob, Pisé and Stabilised Earth*. Country Life, London, 1947.

SOURCES OF INFORMATION

Specialist advice on the conservation and repair of clay and cob buildings in Britain can be obtained from:

The Society for the Protection of Ancient Buildings, 37 Spital Square, London E1 6DY.
English Heritage, 23 Savile Row, London WIX 1AB.
Cadw (Welsh Historic Monuments), Brunel House, 2 Fitzalan Road, Cardiff CF2 1UY.
Historic Scotland, 20 Brandon Street, Edinburgh EH3 5RA.

All County Councils and some District Councils have Historic Buildings Advisors or Conservation Officers.

Devon Earth Building Association and the *Devon Historic Buildings Trust* can be contacted through Devon County Council, County Hall, Exeter.
EARTHA, the East Anglian equivalent, can be contacted through Conservation Officers of East Anglian local authorities.

Advice on the technology of new earth buildings, particularly overseas, can be obtained from:

Intermediate Technology Development Group, Myson House, Railway Terrace, Rugby CV12 3HT, U.K.
CRATerre, École d'Architecture, 10 Galerie des Baladins, F-38100 Grenoble, France.

The cob manor house of Hayes Barton, East Budleigh, Devon. The chimney formerly displayed the date 1625.